Just Below the Surface

By:

Benny R. Ferguson Jr.

Just Below the Surface
By Benny R. Ferguson Jr.
© 2012 - 2020

ISBN:
978-1-7354117-2-9

Published by:
The Ferguson Company

Editor & cover design:
http://roxanec.wix.com/time-to-read.com

Introduction

There comes a point in life were you begin to question the validity of what can and is possible for you. I know it seems that the older you get, your lot in the world seems to be set. Family is an inescapable chore, and you feel as though your life has to be on hold until everyone else is taken care of. Your current job is not fulfilling or satisfying to the seemingly unquenchable yearn of your inner self. The income level that your current job provides for your life is a far cry from allowing you the life that you once envisioned for yourself and your family.

So what do you do?

Do you give up? Have you given up on the dreams that once danced through your mind just before bed? Have you smothered the fire that burned brightly, fueling your engine through countless years of school, through those countless long nights?

I hope that you can remember those once passion filled visions. I hope you can remember the determination that could not imagine taking no for an answer.

If you can remember, this is not motivation for you to keep trying, this is a way for you to accomplish, and exceed anything you ever thought possible.

In this short work, my goal is not to teach you anything. My goal is to make you aware of something that is already present, a power, a potential that resides within you. A potential that has always existed within each and every human being, and yet we have lacked the proper knowledge and direction to become aware of its existence and workings in our lives.

I invite you to get to know you.

I invite you to get to know the fundamental cause of your life, and to become aware of its workings.

I invite you to begin unleashing the raw infinite potential that lies dormant within you, and if you have ever wondered, the answer is yes;

"Thought Does Matter"

Repeating Experiences

It is time to become aware of the many exciting works and happenings just below the surface of you, of your being, of your life. If you are open to expanding your understanding of you, and becoming aware of the fact that you are creating your life experience with every thought and with every grand or subtle show of emotion, then you are ready to see the effects of one who takes this knowledge and applies it to every area of their life with expectation, wonder and awe.

Just below the surface, you come to realize that your life, to this point, has been a series of repeating experiences. The types of people that you encounter daily, the situations and circumstances of life that seem to be propelling you forward or holding you back, the patterns of your relationships, intimate, friendly, and work related, your finances, your health; your life, to the trained knowing eye is very predictable. You on the other hand, may feel as though it is highly volatile and out of control. This is because you are currently, solely focused on the events of the day, and are not applying wisdom to noticing obvious patterns and asking, "Why?"

This is the reason for this book, this quick note. This book briefly describes, brings to light those happenings that are right in front of all human beings, but because of the focus of our minds, we fail to see and become aware of them.

In your relationships, if intimate, you and your partner have similar disagreements, similar arguments over and over again because your inner ideas of what should and shouldn't be, what is and is not possible, oppose each other. You do not know this is an issue of inner make up, therefore you are doomed to be victims of this circumstance over and over again.

In your relationships, if with friends or colleagues, the disparity between you and these individuals is an issue of mind. It is an issue of your propensity to either see the good in others or the bad. It is your propensity to see what is right or what is wrong. As you might notice, one of these ways of seeing people builds relationship and the other destroys relationship, from the inside out. This is the way it works. This is the way life works.

Whatever you are seeing on the inside of you, whatever you believe to be true, becomes true for you and you meet it in your experience. The source is within you.

So the answer to the riddle, the answer to repeating experiences is that your mind is holding ideas, concepts, and perceptions about the world, and they are very specific. These ideas are just below the surface, not in your thinking mind (conscious mind) but in your subconscious/unconscious mind. These ideas are powerful, and are doing 2 things all of the time, never ceasing, without break, in every area of your life.

1. They are placing you in alignment with your experience, good and bad, through your thoughts, emotions, words and behaviors.
2. They are attracting/drawing the experience to you.

To know what you believe, simply look at what you are experiencing.

Become Aware of Your Thoughts

You must become aware of your thoughts!

Thinking is the second port in a powerful creative mechanism that exists within you. And it exists, just below the surface.

Do you remember what you were thinking at any one point today? If not, there is no way that you will ever begin to link your thoughts of today with the events of tomorrow. This is something you must begin to practice, something you must begin to get good at. This is what opens the doors to understanding and to possibility.

- You think of people and they show up, they call you, they write you, or someone brings them up in conversation.

- You relish a perfect gift, and it shows up from the most unlikely of places.

- You wish you had time, and someone offers you a break.

These types of instances are happening all the time, but because you are not aware of your thinking, of your thoughts today, you do not realize that you were the catalyst to events tomorrow.

What about those "Ah Ha!" moments? The ones you receive when you have been searching for that answer. When and how do they show up? Ah Ha! Moments you want to get to know very well. Through the same process that you get answers, you have tremendous streams of creativity, ideas, and lots of other valuable information available to you that could be worth millions. Are you thinking? No! When you begin to be aware of your thoughts and your thinking you notice that you are not thinking all the time. Often the mind is receiving information just as a radio receiver receives broadcasts. Sometimes it is good stuff and sometimes it is the worst most awful, "Where did that come from!" type stuff. But you were not actively thinking. Become aware!

Those Ah Ha!! moments come when the mind is empty. It is clear you are not consciously thinking and there is no information streaming into it. This is the place where deep meditation takes place, and the place where your Source, the Infinite is able to communicate with you directly, as it is always trying to do.

What were you thinking? Becoming aware of your thoughts reveals another very important point, alignment. You notice that your normal patterns of thought (what you think about), the emotions that you normally feel, how you speak (what you talk about), and how you behave (your actions), are in direct alignment with the **UNDESIRED** situations or circumstances that you experience. There is no way around the responsibility. Everything becomes clear once you start paying attention. Being aware of your thinking begins to open the door.

Become Aware of Your Emotion

The emotion of the human being is what gives energy and life to his/her thoughts. Emotion is a non-physical activity, just like thinking. Emotion manifests itself as tremendous energy, located in different areas of the body. Have you ever paid attention to the feeling when you were getting upset? You can feel the energy rising in your body, just before it overcomes you. You can also feel the energy subsiding, as it dissipates and is released from the body.

You can feel the energy of individuals in a room if things are going well and everyone is excited. You can also feel the energy if there is something wrong.

It is time to become aware of emotion. Emotion is the third port of the creative mechanism that exists within you. It is powerful. It is also meant to be under your control.

For years I have watched so many fall victim to their emotions because they have lived there lives reacting to the situations and circumstances of life, as opposed to proactively charging the ideas of a life desired with the pure energy of emotion.

Let's try a test. Think of something that upsets you at the moment. It can be something that you do not like or something that you disagree with. Close your eyes for a moment and think about it. See it. Relive the conversation about it, and feel the emotion as it begins to rise inside of you.

Now think of a situation that you are excited about, that makes you happy inside. See it in your mind. Hear the sounds. Relive any conversations around it. Feel the emotion as it rises up inside of you.

Now, what happened to the emotion, the energy from the image of what upsets you? It is gone right. What did you change? The only thing that changed was the image that you held in your mind, and if you are aware, you can do that all day long to stay in **ALIGNMENT** with your desired outcomes in life. This is important because you are the catalyst. Your (CIP) Core Inner Processes, the creative mechanism that exists within you, of which your emotions are a part, is the fundamental starting point to your life experience.

Can you believe it? Are you ready to accept responsibility?

If you so you merely have to look in the mirror for permission to act beginning today.

Meeting the Idea

The reigning prevailing dominant ideas that you carry in your subconscious/unconscious mind are your beliefs. They exist as pictures. They are images of a past long gone. Many are images of distant pains and misfortunes that you wish never to experience again, but because they are charged with the energy of emotion, you continue to meet them in life over and over again.

What is your idea of marriage? Is it a beautiful relationship, were husband and wife operate as one team? Are the accomplishments and purposes, goals and dreams of each person carried in the forefront of their partner's mind? Is it a unit whose foundation is built on trust, individuality, honest and genuine friendship?

This sounds good. It is what most say they want, but it is not their true idea of marriage.

Your true idea of marriage is the same as the marriage relationship images you saw when you were growing up. The ones you were closest to. The ones you were emotionally attached and invested in. If you saw broken relationships, arguing, verbal and emotional abuse; these images are now your foundation. These images are the guiding force behind your present thoughts, emotions, and behaviors.

No matter how hard you try not to be or experience the same thing, these are the images that you carry subconsciously, and if you do not address the issue there, you are doomed to experience a repeat, the reflection of the images that you carry.

Remember alignment??

If you were a part of a family in which one of the parents was authoritarian, you have those images in your subconscious as being true, as being what relationship and marriage are like. This is why you continue to experience individuals in relationship who are controlling and attempt to be dictatorial, or who are jealous and full of insecurities and need to control to protect themselves.

You may attract individuals who are not able to make decisions and look to you for guidance because you carry the traits of the authoritarian. Either way, you are and will meet the ideas that you carry subconsciously in your experience.

In your health, eating habits and body functioning as you get older traditionally reflect the rest of your family. We accept this without question.

These images are guiding the functioning of the body. Begin to change the core beliefs, the images/ideas held in your subconscious.

Your finances are a reflection of the level of wealth and comfort that was experienced as a child. Most people are in the same income range as their parents, with few exceptions. This remains the norm until new ideas of success, accomplishment, and abundance are planted, come about by association with others who have achieved more, or some dramatic, abrupt mental shift occurs.

All areas of life are functions of the ideas that are held in the subconscious mind, and each individual is different. My personal experience was and is completely different from my wife's experience. There is no escaping it.

We meet our own dominate ideas in life, and to change our lives we must change the ideas that we carry.

Chasing The Past

Your personal history is what dooms you. It has compiled over the years because no one has told you that your thoughts plus emotion are the aligning/attracting factor in your life. You are chasing the past every time you relive a painful hurt, accident, or mistake. You are chasing the past every time you remind yourself to feel guilty.

Take note that every time you revisit these instances, situations, or circumstances you relive them, mentally, in the present as if they are actually happening. You see the images in your mind. You feel the emotion, the anger, the fear. You then, at some point, talk to someone about how terrible it was and how you couldn't believe that it happened, and in so doing you place yourself in direct alignment with similar type circumstances and events again and again.

The only way to freedom, is to begin to focus on the experiences, the events that you want.

Your mind is your own. You must take responsibility for it. It is a magnificent gift from the Source of all that is, a powerful ally, that will control you if you do not control it.

As it stands, your thoughts are on autopilot. Your thinking is a result of the beliefs that exist presently in your subconscious mind.

Your conscious thoughts are on autopilot.
The vast majority of the time they are in reaction to some stimuli, event that has happened outside of you or to you.

The state of your country's economy does not have to be reflected in your personal economy. Each individual mind is programmed with what is true and what is not by television, radio, friends and family. These are all ideas. They are not true for you, the individual, until you internalize them and solidify them through repetition into you own subconscious mind.

This is how generations and generations of loved ones and family members have been lost to the pains of mediocrity and suffering. They believed the ideas of society. They believed the ideas of those around them, instead of identifying completely and solely with the desires, wants, hopes and dreams that continued to appear and make themselves known inside of them.

It is not a travesty that they were never told that this was true. It is a travesty that they were never shown that this was true. For the truth is in the experience.

Course of Power – The Test

The course of power is the streamlining of focus and will into an ideal that pulls you toward it. This ideal should be the highest vision, the highest version of a life that you can mentally formulate at the moment. This ideal should not take into account any possible limits, any possible challenges, or any possible objections. A key to the course of power is identifying the end result that you want to meet. It is a grand end result, one that may feel just out of reach, but potentially possible.

The break in the old way of thinking is to no longer focus on what seems to be present in the now, and not on what has happened anywhere in the past. The new way of thinking feeling and behaving is solely in line with the situation or circumstance that you want to see materialized or manifest. This involves keeping an inward focus on the horizon. This involves staying focused, from the inside out on the things that you want, on the things that you want to see in your life and no longer giving energy attention or focus to the things that you do not want. All mishaps of the past are forgotten. All mistakes are set free. Guilt, anger, and frustration, which you hold toward yourself or another, are let go. This clears the path for the new. You are the giver of life to the ideas. Your attention to events in the past, give them life in the present and therefore project them into the future, thus assuring that you cross paths with it again and again.

The course of power is setting an ideal for every area of your life. What type of person do you want to be? What type of husband or wife? What type of business person? What type of father or mother? What type of friend? Whenever you come in contact with a situation that has not been set under your umbrella of ideals take a moment and envision what you want it to look like. These are the habits of the masters. You must see what you want it to look like. What do you want the outcomes to be? You are doing it all of the time all ready, just normally in the wrong direction. Normally it is in the direction of what you do not want to happen. What would your life look like if you were to program yourself for success? What would your life look like if you developed the habit of only seeing what you wanted to happen and nothing else? You can do this. You can live life this way, without compromise. You have compromised enough to this point don't you think?

Imagine the possibility.

Replacing the Precious

The precious of so many, are the ideas, the beliefs about life that they hold so dear, that they neglect to see the evidence of something greater just below the surface. In coming into your own, you will begin to see that many of the precious ideas that you believe to be true, that you hold onto for dear life, are really based in fear, and have been given to you. They have been passed along from parents, loved ones and close friends, from which they received the same way. These precious ideas are all a result of reactions to life, or reactions to events that someone else experienced. They are not true reality; they are merely someone else's experience of reality based on their inner makeup which interprets the world, reality in its own unique way.

The terrain of life is malleable. You are able to mold it into what you want to experience, into what you want it to be. This is your present experience. It is based on your dominant ideas (beliefs), your thoughts, your emotions, your words and behaviors. When you begin to change the types of information, the images that flow through and operate in this mechanism, your Core Inner Processes, your experience of life begins to change.

The evidence is all around us. Individuals of middle to upper class mindset can easily become poverty stricken, mentally and in their experience, if they begin to associate with and take on the mindset of individuals who live a poverty stricken life. Why, because through association they begin to believe that the situation they are now seeing is true. The opposite is true as well. Individuals who grow up in poverty stricken areas of the world can change their stars if they begin to hang around individuals of an abundant wealthy mindset. They begin to see opportunities for growth and expansion that they did not see before. They begin to experience levels of health, wealth, and abundance that they did not believe to be possible.

It is all a function of the mind, the mentality of the individual.

The replacing of the precious is obviously required, when you begin to look at the experiences which are no longer serving your higher purpose. You quickly see whether your beliefs, your precious ideas about life, are shiny, shimmering, beautiful gems, or are dull, gray, festering stones, which are causing your life to stall, and are casting a dark cloud across several areas of your life all at once.

That which is most precious to you, should be a vision of life that is beautiful. It should be a vision of life that is powerful. It should be a vision of life that is constantly drawing you to become more than you presently are. That which is most precious to you, is a life that is expanding your limits. It is engaging possibility. It does not compromise with the quality of which is produced.

Finally, that which is precious to you is your own. Hopefully it has not been suppressed too far down because of lack of trust and faith in the fact that life will provide that which you want, need and ask for.

Unknown Impact

Just below the surface, is it possible that your thinking is bubbling, molding, and manipulating your desires into physical form? Is it possible that your thinking is drawing and attracting the necessary resources, the proper assembly of people, to bring your idea into reality? Is it possible that whatever you want in life is simply a matter of vision, belief, and expectation?

Thought has no bounds. The subconscious, unconscious mind is fully and wholly connected to Source, the Infinite, that which you came from and will return, and from that standpoint there is no prejudice, there is no race, there are no objections, there are no rivals, and there is no rejection. There is simply LOVE Unconditional, and to live your life from this standpoint, from this knowing, is Power. Living your life from this standpoint is calm and peace. Living your life from this standpoint frees you from stress, worry, and doubt because you know that what you focus on, give your attention to, and envision clearly in your mind does and will come to pass. You are free.

You are free to live. You are free to grow. You are free to expand, because now you know the unknown impact of your being, of the magnificent gifts that you have been blessed with. It is time to begin utilizing them in the right direction

Coming into play is the empirical act of will and purpose.
Will meaning full expectation and determined effort which propels forward the energy of life into the wants and desires of the individual.

Purpose is whatever the greatest grandest fullest expression of you is at this moment.

Purpose is first found in hindsight. Purpose exists in those attributes and those experiences that brought the highest joy, the highest exhilaration. When looked at closely, all people around you benefited from the joy and exhilaration that you felt. In hindsight you will see those abilities that come natural to you. You will see the way in which you work with other people that is the mutually beneficial. You will see that you have not explored the best way to make income doing that which fully exploits your strengths. You will see that you have not pushed the envelope on what you are capable of. Hindsight can be a great teacher, when you look for the hidden potential, the hidden possibility, the opportunities missed. Hindsight is great for looking ahead and being prepared to seize what is to come.

The unknown impact of you can be revealed in any and all efforts to go contrary to previous ways of thinking and believing. The moment you try to run contrary to who you are right now, you run into the wall of beliefs and images that have prevailed for years. These beliefs and images wonder why you have attempted to disturb after so long. They believe that you have lived in harmony and that there is no reason to change. They have set the body to react and think in habitual ways so that you can focus on other pressing matters. They do not understand that the current path being directed by the present inner habits are no longer serving you. They do not understand that their inner fuel is fear, and that there is a higher octane fuel for life. It is a fuel that propels forward and does not hold back. It is a fuel that is a builder of relationships and not a destroyer. It is a fuel that accompanies ideas of power, of growth and expansion on their journey to manifestation, and does not sabotage them or destroy them while in process.

The unknown impact of you is the hidden secret; it is the hidden message that is spread all around the world, dating back 5000+ years.

The unknown impact of you is the missing piece to the puzzle of your life. The minute you begin to engage this power you begin to feel an inner difference, an inner change, and with time, evidence of your work begins to show.

The Gift of a Lifetime

The gift of a lifetime is knowing that you are connected, inseparable from all that is good. It gives life to and grows the trees. It grows and gives life to all plants and all animals from the smallest to the largest. It provides the information to the smallest of seeds for it to become that which it is meant to be. It provides the fundamental energy and is the source of all inanimate objects; the soil, the rocks, the air, the water. Just as the fish, unknowingly lives and exist within the ocean, so do you exist within your Source, the infinite. Just as the universe, the many galaxies, the many stars, the sun and all the wonders not yet discovered exist within it, so do you exist within it, and simultaneously it exist within you.

Is it a human being, I doubt it. It is the pure essence of life, nothing is outside of it, and besides; to be all things, you cannot be any **ONE** thing. You must be something else. Thus furthers the mystery, but we can concern ourselves with that later.

The gift of a lifetime, is knowing that all energy, all knowledge, all ideas, all abilities, all potential for health, wealth, and abundance already exists within you. You simple must align yourself with it, and it is your responsibility to do this since this is where you came from in the first place. It is the place in which your fundamental being exists right now. So to realign yourself with greatness, with unlimited power and potential, you must envision and become it from the inside out.

Notice the innocence, the beauty, the strength of a tree. It just is, without choice, and is secure in its alignment with its Source, unconcerned with whether it will eat or drink, or be provided for in any way.

Notice the innocence, the beauty, the strength of a flower. It just is, without choice, and is secure in its alignment with its Source, unconcerned with whether it will be provided for.

Notice the animals, secure in their being, confident in their alignment with their Source. Life and death are neither good nor bad. They are merely a function of life.

And then there is you, you have the ability to think. You have the ability to choose, and in so doing, you have strayed from the knowing, strayed from the security, and have become concerned/fearful of whether you will be provided for in the most basic and simplest of needs and desires.

There is no separation between you and all that is. You are a being of light, spiritual, nonphysical, right now. Begin to live from that point, from that knowing. You have a physical body, for a brief moment in time.

The nonphysical faculties of thinking and emotion are the most powerful things about you while you have a physical body.

Begin to live from this point, from this knowing, and watch the changes appear, the effects of this inner shift toward life.

Knowing that you are within the Source of all that is, and that that Source is within you is The Gift of a Lifetime.

Proof of Experience

The proof of experience quickly becomes evident as you begin to reconstruct the foundation of your living.

Living life on the basis of the only control I have is over myself, and that is enough, is the first step.

You cannot control your children, you cannot control your spouse or partner, you cannot control your coworkers, the only control you have is over yourself, and when you begin to exert control over the faculties that exist within your body, the exterior circumstances that you are accustomed to begin to change.

There is no separation between you and your Source, so there is no big or small desire. There is only your thought. You think of something to drink and it is gifted to you. You think of something to eat and there are extras that no one wants to go to waste. You are placed in alignment with events in life by your thought. You are experiencing a certain type of life, or your life is colored, by your thought.

Take inventory, and witness what it is you normally see in the world. Whether you see the challenges in life or the opportunities, the good in people or their personal challenges, is a matter of the lens that your mind's eye is looking at the world through. Whether you notice the good that your children do, and commend and acknowledge them on it, or you notice the mistakes that they make and continue to let them know how they should know better, is a matter of the type of lens that your mind's eye is looking at the world through.

The type of lens that you are viewing the world through is just that, a lens, and it has blind spots, large ones. It is very difficult to see the good when the lens you are looking through only illuminates the bad. It is very difficult to see opportunities when the lens that you are looking through only illuminates the obstacles. It is very difficult to see the courage, the possibility, the potential in our fellow human beings, when the lens we are looking through only allows us to see their faults.

The truth is that it is not difficult at all, because you just do not see them. It is as if they are not even there. The lens does not allow you to see fully and clearly. Your dominant ideas about life create a personal map of the landscape of life, but it is not the real territory. The real territory is virgin land, ready to be explored, cultivated, expanded, multiplied and built upon, but it will not be that for you if you are unable to see it.

A pure, clean lens, through which the mind is able to look out upon life, is free of the major blind spots. It is free of expectation of others. It is free of stereotypes. It is free of judgment, and any preconceived notions.

A pure, clean lens has been dipped in LOVE unconditional. It is curved to opportunity, thankfulness, gratitude and appreciation. It is also curved to the potential for greater personal growth and expansion.

The pure, clean lens however still has blind spots. The remaining blind spots are the invisible ideas of what more is possible. These blind spots are removed as you come in contact with fellow travelers who have achieved heights of accomplishment or success that you have yet to believe are possible for you.

The proof of evidence has shown itself long before you have cleared your lens. The minute you begin to observe and remember your thoughts, the obvious relationship between your personal thought and the events in your life will become known.

There is no mistaking it. You are powerful. You have infinite potential. The world is your playground. You merely have to remember.

It's All Just Below The Surface.

Benny Ferguson Jr.

About Benny

Benny Ferguson Jr., once a weary traveler, feeling completely helpless to life, has suffered paralyzing fear, low levels of self-worth and depression, and contemplated suicide. He has attempted and failed, time after time, to achieve and succeed in his finances, his health, and his personal relationships, but always fell victim to unknown fears, self-sabotaging behaviors, limits and barriers.

His personal struggle culminated in 2005, with him waking up at 1:30 am in an anger rage. He woke up after a fear based dream, similar to the ones he had experienced dating back to elementary school. From that point he knew that there was more to life than he had previously been taught and ever knew was possible.

His search for an understanding of who he was, what he was capable of, and how to correct the unknown fears and barriers within, led him to the major spiritual traditions of the world (Teachings of Jesus, Buddhism, Hinduism, The Tao, Islam), branches of Psychology, and to Quantum Physics.

The Result:

"The Diamond Mind Approach…"

where Benny ventures to explain and help human beings become aware for themselves (REMEMBER), that each individual is creating their own life experience through the images they hold as beliefs (unconsciously), their thoughts and their emotions.

Through acute observation, it is obvious that life is being lived from the inside out, and the moment we begin to live life from this understanding we realize that it is true.

Leadership ~ Organizational Culture ~ Customer Experience ~ Sales

"Maximizing Human Performance and Potential By Commanding the Mind"

Question: What is the most important part of an organization?
Answer: The individual

Question: Do processes exist and operate prior to skill and behavior?
Answer: Yes

Question: What are the lost/forgotten determinants to performance?
Answer: Inner workings of the mind

Question: What do these processes consist of?
Answer: Images/pictures, sounds, feelings, tastes, smells, and self-talk

Question: What is the most powerful choice?
Answer: A singular focus on desired outcomes with only consideration for their success

Question: What is the result of this extreme focus?
Answer: Attraction of needed resources, acquiring of necessary skills; revealed inner blocks, revealed limiting ideas and beliefs that you hold about yourself, others, and what is possible

Question: Do I influence my life experiences and the successful completion or accomplishment of my highest goals and objectives?
Answer: Yes, all experiences are grandly influenced by their human participants

Question: Who is most influential?
Answer: The person who is most congruent or in alignment with their desired outcome

Question: Does the experience and performance of an organization have a determinant?
Answer: Yes, the cumulative mind and expectation of the whole

Question: Can the cumulative mind of an organization be controlled?

Answer: Yes, the continuous modeling and communication of the organization's purpose and vision by its Leadership, coupled with the continuous sowing of the images, in the team, of the behaviors and types of performance that yield the desired results

The Diamond Mind Approach...
E – Establish Ideal ~ P – Purify Mind ~ M – Master Senses

What You Learn, What You Gain:

- Learn to create ideals in and around your life, that dictate who you choose to be and how you perform

- Understand, become aware, and experience the processes at work within each human being that dictate behavior and performance

- Ability to dictate how you respond and behave in all situations

- Ability to program desired outcomes, and remain in alignment with them from the inside out

- Ability to identify limiting beliefs and emotions associated with undesired experiences

- Ability to call upon prepared and predesigned images that propel you into powerful mental and emotional states

- Release of stress, doubt, worry and fear

- Commanding presence and influence within your organization and abroad

- Heightened awareness to solutions

- Heightened creativity

*Each individual mind, crystalized around ideal experiences and results, accompanied with the necessary guiding ideas and beliefs dictates the behaviors necessary for powerful performance.

*Increased profits, exceptional customer service, and a powerful work environment are staples of an organization operating from the premise of a Diamond Mind.

About The Ferguson Company:

The Ferguson Company is emerging as a world leader in reminding human beings of their limitless power and potential.

Whether in an individual setting, as a business, or the grand operation of a large organization, the mind of the individual is the fundamental starting point to all behaviors and all experiences. **The inner workings of the mind are the Points of Power.**

Alignment is the lost consideration. In approaching desired outcomes, goals, and objectives, is the mind solely focused, through and through, on that end? Are the thoughts, emotions, words and behaviors of each individual involved in sync, in alignment with that end?

It is possible to cancel the clutter, release all limiting beliefs and ideas, and cultivate an inner, laser like focus that produces a level of performance that will not be denied. It is possible to claim results and outcomes before they appear in outer physical experience.

These are all forgotten attributes of the human being.

The Diamond Mind Approach is a guiding premise, with three comprehensive operatives:

E – Establish Ideals
Generate images of the most desired outcomes or experiences. Create these images in their most perfect form, engaging all of the senses.

P – Purify the Mind
Begin process of installing powerful, driving ideas and beliefs, while simultaneously becoming aware of and replacing all limiting ideas, beliefs and emotional blocks that are already present within the mind

M – Master Senses

Recognize that all outer, physical experiences are effects and not causes. Therefore all less than desirable outcomes are no longer looked at as failure, but feedback. This feedback warrants inner adjustment, until the behaviors and performance that is displayed yields the desired outcomes.

Whether improved individual performance is desired, or the complete overhaul of an organization, *The Diamond Mind Approach* addresses the core foundation to behavior, performance and experience. *The Diamond Mind Approach* addresses mindset, the only area of a human being that precedes skill.

If you or your organization is truly ready to realize your limitless power and potential, then you must learn to master the mind.

Connecting With Benny:

Facebook: www.facebook.com/bennyrfergusonjr

Youtube: www.youtube.com/BennyFergusonJr/videos

Twitter: www.twitter.com/BennyRFergusonJ

Contacting Benny:

Initial contacts to Benny for discussions, interviews, one – on - one or group coaching, speaking or training may be made through telephone or email.

Phone: 336-546-7142

Email: BennyFerguson@TheFergusonCompany.com

LOVE

www.ingramcontent.com/pod-product-compliance
Lightning Source LLC
Chambersburg PA
CBHW021922040426
42448CB00007B/871